Marc

To all the readers of
Private Eye who drew the
Pseuds to our attention.

Published in 1973 by
Private Eye Productions Limited,
34 Greek Street, London W1.

Designed by Peter Windett.

First printed 1973
Reprinted 1975

SBN 233 96446 0

Printed by A. Wheaton & Company, Exeter

PRIVATE EYE'S

BOOK *of* PSEUDS

A MOOD STATEMENT

Drawings by MARC

MCXIIIVXII

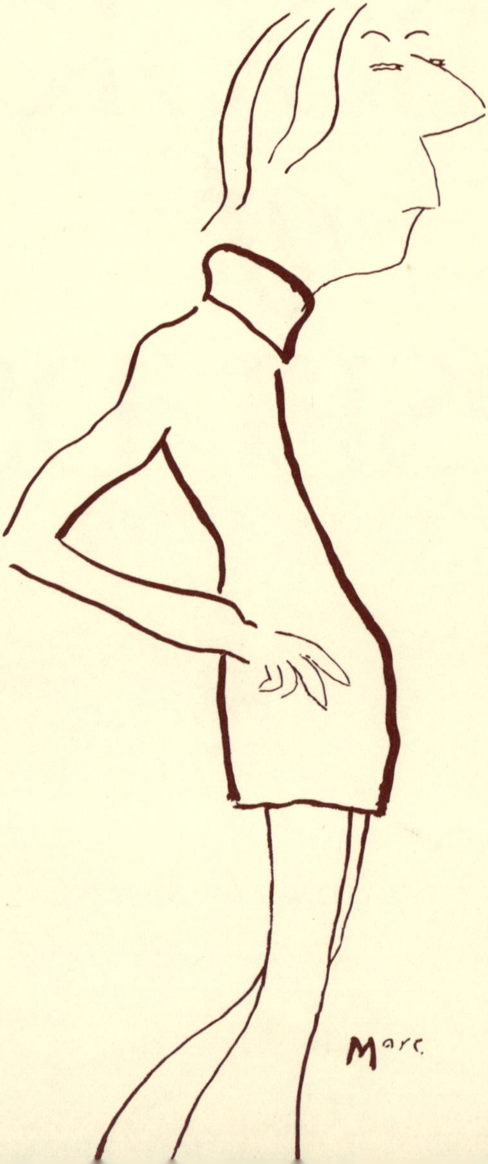
Marc.

What is a Pseud?

The question reverberates in the mind like a pebble thrown unexpectedly into a still moonlit pool, sending ripples towards an undefined circumference.

Certainly there is nothing new in the phenomenon. The poet Swinburne, for example, was once asked by a lady to listen to "a very ancient little Florentine air" that had recently been discovered. She sat down at the piano and played Three Blind Mice. After it was over the poet said it captured perfectly "the cruel beauty of the Medicis".*

It would, I feel sure, be easy to find many equally delightful paradigms in the annals of literature and the arts.

What I have tried to do in assembling this *pot-pourri* is to provide clues towards a tentative definition of pseudery and at the same time to evoke the unique ambience of the contemporary ethos by juxtaposing differing facets of our socio-cultural syndrome.

R. I.

* *At the Pines* by Molly Panter Downes (1971)

CONTENTS

All the following extracts are genuine. Most of them were sent in by readers of Private Eye and reprinted there in Pseuds Corner, 1968–1972.

There will be a distinct period touch about the new book on Mary, Queen of Scots from Dr Roy Strong, director of the National Portrait Gallery, and his wife, designer Julia Trevelyan Oman.

It is, says Dr Strong, a "mood statement" rather than a detailed biography, printed in indigo on pale indigo paper and covered with 16th-century French decoration.

Londoners Diary
Evening Standard

Marc

ACADEME

Concern about physical development–whether irregular menstruation or hair follicles on the scrotum – may mask an underlying anxiety about apparent failure to succeed in academic competition.

Alexander Gunn *New Society*

At present the university's role in acculturation and socialization is the promulgation of the utter mystification of 'corporate consciousness'.

Carl Davidson *Student Power* (*Penguin*)

The radical alternative we seek to the University's present commitment must be a non-absorbable, unifying conceptualisation which will provide political cohesion, both in the short and in the long range, for our programmes and our activities; it must concretise our revolutionary socialist roles without limiting on any levels of specificity our explorations and articulations of concrete mediations of oppression and injustice.

The 1/- *Paper*

Harvey Sacks, a sociologist with an uncanny sensitivity to linguistic behaviour, demonstrated that a conversation is a highly structured event and the rules of sequence organisation in conversations can be formally described. Several years of careful study of conversations have paid off in the discovery of many subtle aspects of this speech event . . . In his presentation at the conference, he argued that conversations can be characterized in terms of two general principles towards which participants always orient themselves.

1. At least one and no more than one person talks at a time.
2. Speaker change recurs.

Joel Sherzer *Language Sciences*

Most people in queues apparently consider that a long wait allows them to leave their place for a short time and ask a neighbour to look after it if necessary. If a coat or chair is left to mark a place in the queue, Dr Mann considers that this is "symbolism reminiscent of burial customs of the ancient Egyptians."

The Times

ADVERTISING

Stallion is the wild one. A wisp of smoke in the air - a camp fire for the shepherds - the smell of smouldering charcoal and the taste of aristocratic wines.

A body-hugging cotton jersey thoroughbred, tamed by Peter Golding in natural colours inspired by the Camargue, Europe's prairie of proud men and noble horses. Cool-groomed girls can wear the small size. A shirt made to the finest quality standards in style and finish – should be washed carefully by hand or machine.

Sales tag on *Stallion* Shirts

Miss Lentheric was created by French perfumers with love in mind. Your first impression of it will be a complex of bergamot, lemon, coriander and Ylang Ylang blended with modern green notes. After you have worn it for a while, its "heart" will appear - jasmine, oriental roses, carnation and muguet. This in turn will be succeeded by long lasting base notes of sandalwood, vetivert, patchouli and ambergris, enhanced by natural musk and civet.

Miss Lentheric Perfume

A chair is a machine for sitting on. No, it's more. It's a piece of double-think in which ambivalence is ensnared like a fly in amber. It is conflict: vertical emphasis versus horizontal function. It is morality: an autobiographical comment on the designer's attitude to relaxation.

It is a philosophical dichotomy: required to be positive in trinity. It must say what it has to say and do what it has to do whilst being what it has to be. So how can a chair be witty and elegant and *make a fresh statement about its purpose?*

The Epsom combines a series of rhythmic interacting curved forms which yield without changing. It takes a sophisticated plain material, or leather, real or man-made, and contrasts it with the satin-smooth arrogance of highly machined surfaces.

William Plunkett Ltd.
Publicity Handout

How do you give a hint of sexual promise to a bath product without verging on bad taste - or the ridiculous? This was the problem facing Allen Brady and Marsh when it started work in the 1969 campaign for Badedas bath additive.

The answer it came up with was – fantasy. But then it had to find out how to use it properly and how to find a link between the fantasy of the "sexual promise" and the realism of the bath.

The first few approaches they tried didn't work. "We took a bath into a field (mentally)," says art director Al Waldie, "and conjured up lakes, with a man and a woman reflected in them. We also tried showing a naked bloke and a woman who would have been the original Adam and Eve, but it didn't work."

"We even went through a pop art phase," says creative director Roderick Allen. "We showed a girl in a bath with Arabian knights galloping about - just like a twenties movie poster. There would have been an obvious association between the girl in the bath and the situation, but not a meaningful one."

Mary Ann Hildrew *Campaign*

But, more than this, the traditional method of sealing off the top of the pack produced a closure that could only be opened destructively and couldn't be resealed. So eating crisps was an invitation to product-sadism. You tear the pack open to get at the contents, rip it further to get at the corner-lurkers in the bottom, and then crush it crackling-flat in the fist before throwing it away. It's the first and most familiar of Total-Destructo products and probably sublimates more aggression per annum than any quantity of dramaturgical catharsis.

However you look at it, or listen to it, the total relationship of crisp to package is a deafening symbiosis that comes near to perfection. And it's the kind of perfection that not even a towering genius could have invented from scratch. The neatness of the relationship has almost a vernacular quality about it, like some survivor from a lost golden age of peasant technologies that have matured long in the wood and hand: the oar, the axe, the rolling pin.

Reyner Banham *New Society*

To be fair, though, there are one or two moments in the current crop of chocolate gobblers and washing power fixated mums that are genuinely imaginative. I like the lady in the bath with sides which turn into waterfalls; and really beautiful is the golden crisp commercial most of which is shot from inside the bag.

George Melly *The Observer*

Man 25. 45 shirts have been unashamedly designed for Achievers, capital A.

Men in the prime-time of life.

Prime movers with power who know how to wield it.

Men with the charisma that goes with success.

The kind of men who enjoy the journey as much as the destination . . . the kind who, rather than waste their Aston at the legal limit on M1, save its visceral performance for the unrestricted pleasures of the Autostrada del Sol. Some men.

But then, Man 25. 45 are some shirts.

Advert *Sunday Times Colour Magazine*

It looks as if everyone connected with Bowyer's advertising has fallen in love with that phrase "The posh sausage". Understandably. It cropped up again this week in a gorgeous commercial for Spartan's Pork pies, There was just the pie, taking up most of the screen, and a large knife. To background strains of Bach-type music, the knife sawed back and forth through the pie, tilting and dipping like a violin bow as the music swooped and soared. Only after the mellow conclusion was there a voice. And it said, simply: "From the makers of the posh sausage . . . . . a rather noble pork pie." Great, really great.

John Monday *Campaign*

ARCHITECTURE

The design of movement – what an obvious concern for an architect in our hot-rod century, and what a sadly neglected concern! "The house was designed to be one complete space," the McNultys have said, "a stream of circulation off which different areas develop for eating, sleeping, entertaining. Many spaces, however, are not defined; rather, they become important psychologically and aesthetically as pauses, hesitations within the general movement." A stream of circulation and a stream of consciousness: "One can see this intention materialised in the walls whose separate yet related curves open and close one's sight-lines, yet reveal continuous vistas wherever one moves."

Peter Blake *Daily Telegraph Magazine*

To sit in the reconstructed entrance of Montparnasse-Bienvenue metro station watching projections of Guimard's main architectural achievements while listening to a record of piano-music by Satie is one of the sublest pleasures Paris has to offer the visitor this season.

Jeffery Daniels *The Times*

One day he was exploring the country round the River Lot when he noticed a shop. "I was driving along through this village - it was a pretty little spa called Miers. I rather like spas and drinking all those waters. Then I saw the shop.

It was absolutely banal suburban French architecture, but it stood alone and I felt it had an incredible kind of purity."

David Hockney quoted in *The Observer*

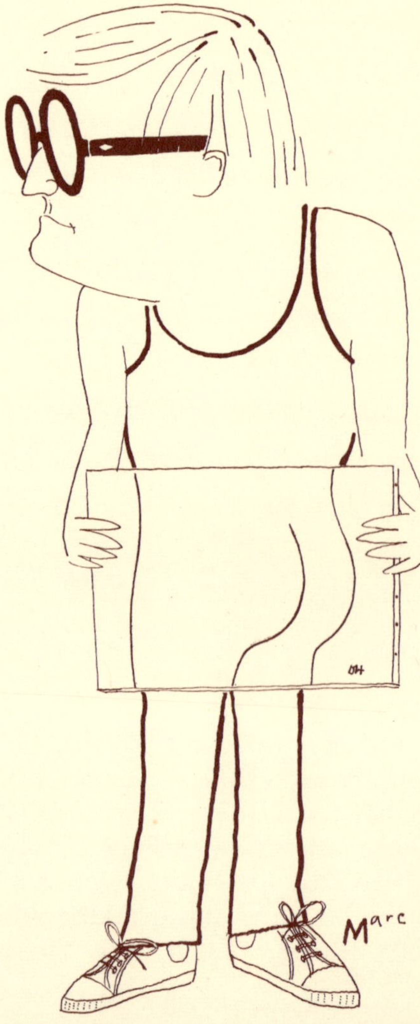

When (Robin) Welch moved into the Stradbroke Farmhouse he noticed the pipe junctions that had been rejected. They were lying where the plumbers had left them in the grass. He recognised their intrinsic beauty and determined to give them a proper place in the cultural scheme of things. Now they stand in the clean surroundings of the Craft Centre looking intentional and delicately balancing Welch's ceramic burnt-out balls on their heads.

Sheldon Williams
Art & Antiques Weekly

'ART'

Ian Nairn's creed is simple. He says: "I think we're here to try to make masterpieces of one sort or another. They don't have to be fine-art or difficult - one of today's troubles is that there are far too many people trying to paint or write plays – but somehow, somewhere, we must twist the tail of existence. Maybe in a meal, or in a marriage, or even in the way in which you ask for a bus ticket."

Radio Times

A vivid experience for me was going to King Arthur's Seat one evening at the moment when a great orange balloon of Graham Stevens's rolled very slowly down the mountain. Its relation to the site and the elements was majestic and needed no explanation.

Guy Brett *The Times*

I have heard of only one poetic mode that seems entirely original. A sometime student at the Royal College of Art chose a precise point in space - the halfway marker on a Dutch dyke and a precise instant in time - say, half past four on a specific afternoon. Having defined these unique, unrecapturable coordinates, he arranged for another human being, a friend, to meet him at the exact given intersection of these arrows of time and place. He termed this meeting a work of art, a totally controlled modification of reality, involving the deviser and the respondent in a collaborative creation. There is something haunting to the project: a sense of the poem as the creation of a total setting, as the momentary imposition of arbitrary order on inchoate possibility.

George Steiner
Times Lit. Supplement

Fluorescent Crysanthemum is a pleasant exhibition to walk round. A carefully hidden loudspeaker system diffuses concrete music over the whole space, right at the entrance a slide-projector throws the concise insignia of the ancient Japanese aristocratic families at your feet on the white floor, there's a section of posters mounted on the facets of cubes glued to the ceiling, a darkened section of electronic sculpture, their perfectly wired systems enclosed in perspex, and a section of cloth kite-sculptures mounted on walls with cloud projections sailing over them.

Guy Brett *The Times*

Marioni's own earliest "sound piece" (which, incidentally, held an unseen time element since it involved drinking beer all afternoon beforehand) was the act of urinating into a galvanised bucket from the top of a ten-foot ladder.

Cordelia Oliver *The Guardian*

The largest work in Richard Long's exhibition at the Whitechapel Gallery takes up the whole ground floor, and may only be looked at over a barrier. It is an immense X-shaped cross made of pine-needles strewn on the floor. From a distance this material takes on a density almost of pencil-shading. For all its fleeting insubstantiality, a German collector who owns a work made of the same material and has installed it on his lawn, is said to collect it up needle by needle in plastic bags every time the grass has to be mown.

Guy Brett *The Times*

In his new premises at 41 Sloan Gardens, Nigel Greenwood has a kind of workshop show by two artists. One is far from conceptual. Keith Milow is exhibiting a new series in which he continues his hide-and-seek with that sharp arrow-like form which comes and goes through his work like a ghost. But the other, a young American artist called Joel Fisher, can safely be given the new label; his pieces consist of scraps of "paper" rendered down from clothing, and a stack of blocks of yellow soap made, believe it not, out of best butter. Mysterious but not mystic, they seem to have something to do with organic substances changing personality.

Nigel Gosling *Observer*

Some amusing and inventive objects are contributed by Hugh Davies, who is really a musician. Using consistently the device of amplification, he brings the tiny scratchings and scrapings of everyday objects up to a level where they absorb your attention. One of his "instruments" - all plastic - is made from a bread-bin (of the kind whose top slides open, not unlike a piano) with plastic spoons as keys inside fixed to upturned tea cups. He also reveals how one can hear extraordinary latent depths of sound of minutely different qualities in any old vibrating piece of scrap-metal by attaching two strings to it, winding these round one's fingers, and putting one's fingers in one's ears.

Guy Brett *The Times*

He collects thousands of old shoes, sprays them silver and scatters them in a trail across the landscape: Hungerford Bridge was one site, and the Bradford moors another.

The effect of the shoe sculptures is fragile but moving because through cast-off waste one wonders about the people who wore the shoes and where their steps led them; and because the sprayed paint is both glamorous and tawdry it makes the lives of those people seem both pathetic and brave.

Keith Dewhurst *Guardian*

A smell of cabbages hung over Glebe Place in Chelsea last week. Not the rank kind which seeps up from basements but the nutty tang which flows off a field of kale in the country. Inside Nigel Greenwood's studio gallery, there they were - captive in rows of crates, subtly green, blobby, tumescent and alive like patches of Rembrandt pigment under the microscope.

The crates made a severe shaft the length of the room, their heads bonded into one corner by two geometrical platforms, their toes linked by a sharpish join to a worrying thing, a makeshift dais made from a fork-lift platform coated with graphite grease to which an automobile engine had been tightly bound, its blackened form nastily suggesting amputation and burning. To the side of it, and joined by a trailing coatsleeve, lay a pile of old clothes in which light-bulbs nestled like eggs or lice or precious stones. A severe addendum to this peninsula lay a little off-shore – three wooden beer palettes, one bare, one covered, one supporting a whirring fan.

It was all very precise and formal, lightly marked out on the floor with chalk outlines, and the next join was tidy, too – another crate tilted on its edge and leading to the heart of the whole arrangement, a sloping trestle covered with hessian on which streams of musky pinkish fluid bubbled and gouted from a metal contraption, staining the cloth and gathering in a puddle at the base like the thin blood of a machine.

I have seen few pieces which filled a big space more satisfyingly.

Nigel Gosling *The Observer*

Boyle, 35, says: "The whole idea of this exhibition is to show just how beautiful ordinary things like roads can be when they are presented in the right way.

"When I put on a light show recently, projecting various things on the screen, I showed microscope pictures of catarrh. It is a way of discovery that things like catarrh are beautiful. A priest told me after seeing that projection that catarrh was like a prayer."

Daily Mirror

ASTRONAUTS

They have gone. To the Moon. Three teardrops of flesh and organism and soul slipping down the face of our world and into the nocturne of God knows where, by God knows what means. They slipped off the Earth on a machine just one hour ago and I watched them fall. God help us all.

John Pilger *Daily Mirror*

THE BEATLES

The best songs (*Beatles Double LP*) for me are the love songs in which lyrical pentatonic innocence is modified but not destroyed by rhythmic ellipsis or harmonic ambiguity.

Wilfred Mellers *New Statesman*

The death and resurrection of heroes appears to be as important to the generation that worships rock as it is to the tribes that celebrate the demise and return of various vegetable gods. Whether the McCartney death is purely physical or metaphorical or even metaphysical, it is very probable that there is more than a little of the mythic logic of the Cambridge school of classical anthropology involved in the Paul-Messiah myth.

J Marks *New York Times*

It must be the hardest thing in the world to be Paul McCartney.

Tony Palmer *Observer*

The concert, billed as "Alchemical Wedding" was organised by Arts Laboratory. One of the co-producers, Jim Haynes, an American, told me before it started that it meant "whatever you want it to mean." Everyone would be taking part.

At the beginning of the concert, which started half an hour late, joss sticks were handed out and twigs and blooms sustained the "flower-power" image. Members of the audience were invited to do such things as stare at their neighbours.

The concert began when a shoeless, bearded man invited us to "listen to this room." Deliberate interruptions followed. It was not long before a contrived hysteria was mounting as the tempo of the music increased.

The final "happening" of the evening was the Beatle John Lennon and Yoko Ono climbing into a white bag in the centre of the stage and writhing.

The Daily Telegraph

If there is still any doubt that Lennon & McCartney are the greatest songwriters since Schubert . . .

Tony Palmer *Observer*

BOOKS

Violence, homosexuality and the spiritual emptiness of post-war Japan characterise these remarkable volumes.

Advertisement *Penguin Books*

Robert Liddell's new novel *Stepsons*, although dealing with simple domestic drama - the long running battle between a woman of this kind and her husband's two boys by a previous marriage - provides us with something more; something significant in terms of English social history. Having read it I found myself wondering about the part played by penis-envy in the building of the British Empire. Paul Scott *The Times*

Forster was not Proust; he was not Joyce; he was not Gide. On the other hand he was not Virginia Woolf and he was not D H Lawrence.

Sir Denis Brogan *Spectator*

I tried to get Wodehouse into perspective. He was on the verge of 90; he was born, therefore, when Proust was only 10.

Michael Davie *The Observer*

HUMAN FUTURISTICS, to be published July 1971, is one of the first books to discuss the *cultural* aspects of futuristics. It explores new concepts of cultural discontinuity, metatransition, transcendence, heterogenization, dehierarchization, symbiosis, polyocular vision, antientropic process, ethnogenesis, anticipatory democracy, and transepistemological education.

Social Science Research
University of Hawaii

It is almost begging the question to point out that while the book examines and implicitly attacks middle-class life, here is Miss Dunn living to all intents and purposes just such a life. "Yes, and I sometimes feel almost total despair about it and want to run off and live in Siberia with Solzhenitzyn and chop wood for him and have his babies in a little room."

Nell Dunn *The Guardian*

Bertie Worster (*sic*) and Jeeves get into hilarious scrapes, have some spiffing times getting the better of cads, but their existence is posited on the existence of Crown and Colony, of hereditary wealth and milito-aristocratic oligarchies of meticulous gradations of rank and tenure.

John Jordan *Hibernia*

I was sitting upstairs in the Cafe Royal with Stephen Spender when the news reached us that Auden and Isherwood had departed to America. I burst into tears.

Michael Nelson *Guardian*

Malling is a shy, 43-year-old picture-restorer, who lives in the depths of rural Suffolk and shuns the town. He has already written 10 novels and 13 plays. His first published fiction, "Dodecahe," is due from Allison-Busby in a month's time.

"How to describe it," Allison mused. "Intense? Convoluted? Hectic? Messy? It is set in a real world, which has somehow become mythical. Icelandic almost.

"The heroine is expelled from a convent after 19 years, accused of Lesbianism though she was only playing leapfrog. She becomes an attendant in a lavatory used by prostitutes and perverts, the natural prey of every freak and outcast. I suppose the nearest comparison would be to Nathanael West. Malling is really asking: What would happen to Jesus Christ today if he were a woman?"

Alan Brien *The New York Times*

CARS

Grand Prix cars are very close fitting - you put them on, more or less, as you would a glove. You wear the car. The car is an extension of yourself. It's almost as if you were a painter, your car the brush, the track the canvas. You go out and paint your pictures on the tracks of the world in the way your character dictates. And it is through these pictures that you reveal yourself to the public for what you really are.

Graham Hill *Observer Review*

Getting back into a Mini after some years of not having driven one is like crawling back into the womb.

Judith Jackson *Sunday Times*

The point about the Wankel engine is not just that it is simple, light and compact. The sheer sensual pleasure of the first rush up through the gears, the subdued growl, something close to turbine smoothness and the instant response that the turbine can never provide; these are things calculated to stick in the mind like the memories of the first run in a Lamborghini.

Gordon Wilkins *Observer Colour Supplement*

Charles Symmonds has promised he'll try to get to the opening of an art exhibition at the New Arts Lab next week, because the items on show have been borrowed from his knacker's yard, Motor Crash Repairs, 265B Finchley Road, London. "They don't appeal to me as art," says Symmonds. "I detest cars. But maybe it's a good idea to show crashed cars. It's frightening. It frightens me."

He has hired out a smashed Pontiac, an A60 and a Mini, to J G Ballard, the science fiction writer, who is showing them in an Atrocity Exhibition. This is what Ballard says it is all about: "Each of these sculptures is a memorial to a unique collision between man and his technology. However tragic they are, I believe that automobile crashes play very different roles from the ones we assign them. Behind our horror lies an undeniable fascination and excitement, most clearly revealed by the deaths of Jayne Mansfield and James Dean, Albert Camus and John F Kennedy. The 20th century has given birth to a vast range of machines – computers, pilotless planes, thermo-nuclear weapons – where the latent identity of the machine is ambiguous. An understanding of this identity can be found in a study of the automobile, which dominates the vectors of speed, aggression, violence and desire. In particular, the automobile crash contains a crucial image of the machine as conceptualised psychopathology. Apart from its function of redefining the elements of space and time in terms of our most potent consumer durable, the car crash may be perceived unconsciously as a fertilising rather than a destructive event – a liberation of sexual energy - mediating the sexuality of those who have died with an intensity impossible in any other form. In 20th century terms the crucifixion would be enacted as a conceptual car crash. The car crash is the most dramatic event we are likely to experience in our entire lives apart from our own deaths."

Back to Mr Symmonds: "I fully agree with all that."

Atticus *Sunday Times*

The inevitable difficulty in treating cars as if they were works of art, instead of expressive objects which exist–

rightly enough—outside the conventional context of the 'fine arts' is that they demand absolute participation. They are if you like environments or Happenings. They do not sit on a wall or a floor: they don't really begin to exist as cars until you get into them and drive because, as McLuhan would put it, they are extensions of one's nervous system.

Robert Hughes *Sunday Times*

CHILDREN

During the child's learning to walk and to talk to say "no" to the mother, to join with the mother to form a potting couple, not only is the child swept up in the great rush of humanization that goes far beyond the pot, but the mother as well is given an opportunity to replay some of her own feelings associated with learning autonomy and individuation, and indeed with enjoyment of defecation and ownership of one's bowels.

Paul Adams *Children's Rights*

CLOTHES

Diana Mac Kimoto makes delicious bits of plastic food jewellery. It all started as a promotional idea when she made little plastic ice-cream cone sculptures as visiting cards for herself. Everyone loved them and wanted to wear them. So the idea of food jewellery happened. Food jewels come as a ring, pendant, cuff-link, brooch or just as a sculpture. Apart from those shown here Diana makes open-faced sandwiches, meals on a plate, e.g., gammon steak and peas, egg and bacon. *Nova*

As our world moves from hardware to software the miniskirt is a major effort to reprogramme our sensory lives in a tribal pattern of tactility and involvement. Nudity istelf is not a visual so much as a sculptural and tactile experience.

Marshall McLuhan *The Observer*

Malcolm Raines makes hats for women like another man would give roses. It's a way of showing appreciation.

"Whenever I see a girl's face I like," he says, "I imagine her in a hat."

Malcolm has nicknames for his favourites: "Bognor, 1928" is a sea hat, all in aqua-green suede, decorated with a sea-spray of wavy feathers, shells and a dangle of suede seaweed. A black velvet Garbo hat, sewn with an enormous jet bead flea on a pink lead, he calls affectionately "Pet Flea." It's dedicated to his girl friend, Alvinia, a 6ft black model. Inside he's sewn "With every stitch a kiss – Malcolm." Every artist signs his paintings.

Fashion Forum *E. Standard*

INDUSTRIAL RELATIONS

All audits tend to be the same (if one may paraphrase Borges), but there is not a day, even in industrial relations, which does not bring surprises, which is not a translucent network of minimal surprises. Innis MacBeath *The Times*

CRITICS

An aesthetic which erases society necessarily precludes a concept of temporality. A historical sociology of art – the examination of its concrete mode of production – is a condition of its differential intelligibility. The 'psychology' of art is ultimately an interdiction of its meaning.

Perry Anderson
Student Power (*Penguin*)

The inevitability of the finest pictures resides in the fact that these are self-framed in an extra aura of heightened meaning by their combination of emotional, social and psychological factors frozen in the precision of the underlying rectitude of geometric placement. The value and significance of the picture finally taken derives from a fusion in crisis of these elements; the ultimate image, snapped at the peak of choice, is fixed through a complex chemistry of moral and muscular explosions, like an orgasm.

Lincoln Kirstein
Photographs of Cartier-Bresson

The attempt to involve Flanagan in an antithetical art historical debate has metamorphosed his sculpture into pawns in a game of stylistic chess, the terms of reference for which are delineated verbally and textually rather than through any meaningful retinal dialectic with the works themselves.

Peter Fuller *Connoisseur*

Exactly *what* use we shall need to make of our phylogenetically programmed capacity for shamanic experience is anyone's guess, though, like Roszak, I don't think psychedelics and do-it-yourself Tantrism are likely to take us far.

Alex Comfort *Grauniad*

Observe this idea of silence as an honourable and creative act. Surely it is related to the lengthening pauses in music from the late Debussy, Webern, and today in their main heir, John Cage. It is related, also, to the new eloquent empty spaces which turn up in sculpture and in painting, so that what is missing has a kind of active presence, an active possibility, and silence is not just an evasion. It is a reminder of modesty.

George Steiner *The Listener*

ERRATA

In our issue of *West Africa* of the week ending July 21, in the article by Femi Osofisan on "Soyinka in Paris", there was an unfortunate misprint. Mr. Osofisan had written: "Even Jean Decock of *African Arts* once reported the formicating thrill he experienced from the shock of proximity of these nude torsos . . ." As published, the word "formicating" ("formication: a sensation as of ants

crawling over the skin", Oxford English Dictionary) appeared as "fornicating". We apologise for this misprint, especially to Mr. Decock for any embarrassment he may have been caused. EDITOR

Erratum

Toroidal Stabilized Pinch Formed with Relatavistic Electrons. Charles W Hartman (Phys. Rev. Lett. 26, 826 (1971)).

In the first column on page 827, the word "super-banana" is erroneous, the result of an editorial substitution. The author used the word "hyperbanana," to designate a topological variant of the banana trajectory.

Physical Review Letters

FILMS

She is now starring on her own account in *The Grasshopper*, a film about a girl who lurches through life, never finding happiness.

There is nothing that does not happen to Miss Bisset in *The Grasshopper*. She runs away from home, suffers a broken marriage to a Negro, is beaten up by a crude, self-made tycoon, befriended by a homosexual and turns to drugs.

She becomes a call girl and then a rich man's mistress. Finally, a musician who pimps for her runs off

with all her money, leaving her alone and finished at the age of 22.

"I know so many girls like Christine," Jacqueline Bisset says of the character she plays. "The theme is so modern; so much part of today."

Unity Hall *The Sun*

We are shown shots of an American girl whose business - or hobby - is taking plaster casts of the erect penises of famous men, and these shots of her in action are counterpointed with shots of Stalin from an old Soviet film thus making Makavejev's point that Stalinism turned socialism on to the wrong track, and only more and better orgasms can set it on the right road again.

Richard Roud *The Guardian*

There is a film a few minutes long by Andy Warhol showing a youth being given an injection in the buttocks by a girl. It isn't by any means meaningless. It is a critique of story-line, of the idea that life makes stories. It is the art of the window-watcher. Yes, it's a form; it expresses a reality; there are such people; such sights are seen and have effect.

Thomas Wiseman *Grauniad*

Suddenly our conversation was interrupted by a terrific commotion when a moth as big as a bat fluttered and dived across the lens. All hands went up to grab it, but the poor thing was captive in the pool of light. One of the assistant directors, a big burly man dressed like a Desert Rat including a beret and hob-nailed climbing boots, tried to knock the creature to the ground, stamping, swearing and swatting at it with his hands. Eastwood, who had been standing by quietly watching the scene, suddenly shouted: "Leave it, leave it, they need killers like you in Vietnam." He moved forward, elbowed the assistant director aside, then cupping his hands gently he guided the fluttering moth into the safety of the dark. There was a silence. Meriel McCooey *Sunday Times*

FOOD & WINE

Geales's Fish Restaurant, in Farmer Street (off Bayswater Road) serves first-class fish and chips with a truly comprehensive wine list and a genteel cover charge of 9d. Exceptional ambiance *and a rare opportunity to take cod fillet with chablis or hake and Moet et Chandon.*

Punch

Do you clench your teeth when you see a fine head of celery? It seems to me that anyone who has once bitten into a cream-white stalk of raw celery and enjoyed the brittle breaking of the cell structure under the tooth's attack, followed by a release of cool juices and nutty flavour, must forever after experience an involuntary tightening of the jaws at the sight of this plant.

Skeffington Ardron *Grauniad*

What I like with a simple *al fresco* luncheon is wine of an engaging pink served very cold in a glass jug or big carafe – wine that looks pretty and need not be taken too damned seriously: a sort of popsy of a wine.

Cyril Ray *The Observer*

Nothing is so exquisite as plumed sliced fennel or cauliflower. (Edna O'Brien says she finds even sliced leeks that tendril round her fingers beautiful).

Thea Porter *Harpers/Queen*

There are only three stalks that really count in cooking and of these celery somehow has wintry associations even though it is now available all year round and rhubarb has lost the immature, Lolita-like appeal it has in early spring and moved into a supporting role for summer. But asparagus has so short and unpredictable a season that there is no chance of it being thought boring, or being overlooked, or neglected.

Margaret Costa *Sunday Times Magazine*

A bottle of very pleasant Le Piat de Beaujolais (33s) helped us to forget that our Poussin Grillé à la Diable arrived bathed in a sauce that cried for more zest and fire.

Beryl Hartland *Daily Telegraph*

He split a matchstick in two, so that he could ease the lobster remnants out from the crevices between his teeth, another gesture of making do with the materials at hand: an essential, inherent efficiency.

Tom Hutchinson *Guardian*

Cream is a lovely word in itself, like velvet, satin or Georgina; or perhaps with more adult taste, like Tia Maria or Drambuie. To watch it come silently, slowly from the separator is like the hushed tones of the Rhapsody in Blue *or the slow movement of clouds over a solitary hilltop, silent but for the occasional bleat of a distant lamb.*

C David Edgar *Daily Telegraph*

Her terrine of duck reaches heights of aesthetic as well as gastronomic delight because the duck, boned by Mrs Stevenson herself, the skin packed with the delicious paté and re-formed, is breathtakingly beautiful - perfectly achieved beneath its amber glaze of jelly.

Margaret Costa *Sunday Times*

Do you make love wearing dirty gloves? That's the effect a smelly glass has on a fine wine.

Pamela Vandyke Price *Spectator*

These days, being a vegetarian seems more and more essential if you even pretend to care about anything from pollution and the Third World to Tolkien and The Who.

Jill Tweedie *Grauniad*

FOOTBALL

Football still is, I would argue, one of the few areas of life in which men become deeply involved. The bourgeoisie have opted into this world . . . Hooliganism seen in this perspective takes on a radically different perspective. It is not the reaction of an expropriated and dwindling working class rump, but indicative of a more generalised disaffection from the controls of the other world.

Huw Benyon Dept. of Sociology, Bristol University *New Society*

Those Leeds goals were possessed of the architectural splendour of Wren and the simple, wholly English charm of Constable.

Alan Thompson *Daily Express*

Leeds United . . . 2 Manchester United . . . 1

The bitter malevolence that erupted in the funeral dolourousness of the first half was blessedly relieved, although never expunged in the more intense legitimate conflict of the second.

Arthur Hopcraft *Observer*

The goal was as simple and as impressive as the Parthenon.

Malcolm Winter *Sunday Times*

With 10 minutes left they suddenly were level. Theirs, too, was a beautiful goal: more complicated, more finely ingrained, more liquid and created virtually out of nothing. Here was the poetry of football . . .

Geoffrey Green *The Times*

"One moment weighs like another. Only in retrospect, selection, we say that was the day, the critical moment." So T S Eliot described the tense period at Canterbury before Becket's murder. So, too, must Leeds and Arsenal have felt these last few weeks as their championship battle has moved towards its climax.

James Wilson *Sunday Times*

Chelsea . . . 2 Notts Forest . . . 0

As the timeless second half of this encounter crawled to its untidy close at Stamford Bridge, one at last began to understand the awfulness of eternity.

Max Marquis *Observer*

. . . AND TENNIS

There are times when men respond to the game and to each other in such a way that tennis becomes not merely a game, but a means of expressing the eternal verities.

Rex Bellamy *The Times*

But whoever witnessed, first, Miss Goolagong's conflictless fantasy, and then, a mere 48 hours later, Vlado Perlemuter's inspiration, at once weightless and weighty, in his piano recital at the Cheltenham Festival (relayed on Radio 3), with Mrs King's and Mrs Court's and *Mr Perlemuter's own complications of years ago in between, must have been struck by the unavoidable tragedy of a life in sport as opposed to an artist's life.*

Hans Keller *The Listener*

WOMEN

'Can you imagine what it will be like when I'm old?' She used to go to bed with an artificial hand lit from the inside. 'Whenever I wake up I look at this and I think, "How pure and white and beautiful you are . . . like everyone should be. Not like men." '

Juliet Greco
(as told to Tony Palmer) *Observer Review*

I've never liked Thursday much. It's a sort of mauve-coloured day (Monday being white, Tuesday pink, Wednesday orange, Friday red, Saturday brown and Sunday silver) and there's a nothingness about it that makes it deadly.

Virginia Ironside *Daily Mail*

But come a child, two children, three and the womb is not satisfied. The periods go on and on, an atavistic, antiquated reminder of what? Today, when men may land on the moon and aim their cameras at Venus, I am still below, feet planted heavily on earth, living evidence of some mad plan to populate this planet out of existence, my mindless womb bleeding hopelessly, hopefully – a lunatic and megalomaniac organ, dumb, deaf and blind to need.

Jill Tweedie *Guardian*

"Vanessa (Bell) had a kind of stoical warmth about her, a monolithic quality. . . . . even if she said little there emanated from her an enormous power, a pungency like the smell of crushed sage."

Angelica Garnett
Recollections of Virginia Woolf

I take my vagina wherever I go. It belongs to me and I belong to it.

Irma Kurtz *Nova*

I can never go into Harrods, and meet a friend – and everyone at one time or another wanders glazedly through Harrods – without feeling like Shelley in *Ozymandias*, without re-echoing his marvellous awe in meeting a traveller from an antique land.

Polly Devlin *Vogue*

The night that Alan and Barbara took Mike Nichols and Jackie Kennedy out to Coney Island for supper, Jackie did something that struck Alan as the most civilized and thoughtful and genuinely gracious act he'd ever seen. Someone came over to their table and asked Jackie for her autograph. "No, thank you," Jackie said.

Barry Farrell *Life*

"There was this girl in an exam I was invigilating who sat pitifully doing nothing. When she left she deposited a letter on my desk which

ended: 'Our minds are all so clogged on the dead ideas passed from generation to generation that even the best of us are unable to control our lives.' I burst into tears."

Germaine Greer *Sunday Times*

LOVE

"I would need a hundred volumes to describe him. He is the ocean. He is the sunset. There is no way of describing the desert or the sky. How can you describe anyone who changes all the time? He is such a vast person. He has a huge personality. He is capable of being so many people, of doing so much. How can I encapsulate him in words?"

Elizabeth Taylor on Richard Burton
Woman's Own

In Hollywood a few weeks ago I made a pilgrimage to the house where she used to live on North Bedford Drive. In Beverly Hills I walked through the rooms where she had once walked, and outside on the lawn paid a lover's act of homage.

From now on I shall be able to say: "I once picked a lemon from a tree in Garbo's garden."

Felix Barker *Evening News*

Hugh made no impression on me at all at that time or on subsequent meetings. The day I really remember was years later, after my third child – that was by my first marriage. He was staying at the home of my brother, who was with him at Christ Church. The daffodils were out and the Queen Mother of the Belgians had dropped in. It was simply lovely.

Lady Alexandra Trevor-Roper
Sunday Times

MUSIC

A single phrase of Beethoven, the great discord of the *Ninth Symphony* – let alone the structure of the movement – conveys this illusion to the hearer, of receiving at one and the same time a perfectly logical and precise communication which might be translated straight into Latin, and an instant revelation of the indescribable depths of the universe.

Enoch Powell *The Listener*

I was for some time uncertain about the grotesque throat noises of the reciter-singer, Roy Hart, sounding as much constipated as mad, but the very embarrassment they inspired (cries of "Rubbish" from the back) was a designed part of a harrowing aesthetic experience utterly new and original.

Edward Greenfield *The Guardian*

Beethoven plays the key note, repeats it three octaves down the scale, jumps up to the diminished 7th, then plummets to the key ncte of the dominant 7th. That last note is the bluest note you ever heard - and he wrote it in 1801, 60 years before the American Civil War.

James Greenwood *Daily Mail*

The force behind a Mahler symphony is centrifugal and centripetal at the same time.

Bernard Jacobson
Concert Programme of LSO

The music of *Lament of the Waves*, which became a ballet at Covent Garden on Thursday, is by Gérard Masson (b. Paris, 1936), who has experienced Varèse and Stockhausen. It is an impressionist Debussyish piece, but with newer noises. For instance, there are two bursts of strange muttering, which are the orchestra saying their names and the instruments they play.

Richard Buckle *Sunday Times*

Quite often the experience of the music of Cage and his followers is more rewarding than the music itself – thus Dream (1948), a five-minute piano piece written in the rhythmic structure of a dance by Merce Cunningham (with whom Cage has frequently and very fruitfully collaborated), was played by John Tilbury off stage on the greenroom piano, while Cornelius Cardew sat, immobile, at the grand on the stage. What was important was not so much the distant swirls of what sounded (at 'first glance') like a Chopin nocturne, but the way in which one's ears had to become accustomed to the semi-silence (and to other people's ears becoming etc) as one's eyes do gradually to the dark. (A friend sitting a few rows nearer the stage heard only the Stuttgart Chamber Orchestra from the neighbouring hall.)

Michael Nyman *Spectator*

Surely we have a right to be bored by Bruckner.

Peter Stadlen *Daily Telegraph*

He (Cornelius Cardew) sees no harm in using fragments of the classics to give a point of reference for the player and audience alike. The normal pattern of events is that a work by a member of the orchestra is prepared for performance. The composer specifies the duration of the piece and any planned activities or sounds he may require. He gives a particle of a well-known piece as the germ for the individual player's improvisatory activities. Any action or sound or both is valid as music as long as it is the result of some emotional stimulus and is felt by the player to be necessary to the shape of the work.

Thus the possessor of a packet of sandwiches may feel that eating them is essential to the satisfactory expression of his part in the piece. It is quite possible for a composer to specify that every member of the orchestra eats sandwiches for a given period of time: it is, however, up to the individual as to how he eats the sandwiches to derive the maximum emotional effect.

Gavin Barrett *The Guardian*

SCHERZO by Alan McCombie

The composer writes: Serio-modular formalism, in its most extreme and advanced form, has shown us the

incipient birationalism of total serialism. This dichotomy is explored in the present work through the multiplanar interjuxtaposition of bivalent (quasi-multivalent) tone clusters with neo-aleatoric material arranged in spaced points, occlusions, antipoints and reflexes. The contemporary dilemma concerning the socioeconomic relevance of multiples, i.e. ambidialectic, thematicism, is high-lighted by the organic reantiorientation of paraorganic material throughout the work.

Programme Note *The Prospero Ensemble*

While a student at Manchester University, I wrote a thesis, for my bachelor's degree, on Indian music. Despite its title, borrowed from campanology, the influence of Indian music is very clear in my Stedman Doubles, written at that time 1955 . . . . . Stedman Doubles is a tour de force not only in the obvious technical sense - the extreme difficulty of the writing for instruments, which, in the cadenzas, where the players are 'free', is meant to inspire them to improvise even greater feats of virtuosity – but also a tour de force of sheer concentration for the two performers – as indeed for the listener.

Peter Maxwell-Davies *The Listener*

The one piece that was live, unexpected and uncluttered, was noisily and aggressively received. This was a beautifully poised performance by John Tilbury of, and on, Shozyg I*: the shozyg is an instrument* *devised by Hugh Davies consisting simply of two springs inside a book cover (originally the last volume of an encyclopaedia: SHO-ZYG) activated by tiny means (fingers, screwdriver) and the sound then amplified beyond recognition.*

Michael Nynam *The Spectator*

Easily appreciable dialectically is the contradictory inter relationship between repetition and variants leading to a stepwise process which, with a certain acceleration, gives rise to a chain of more and more radical transformations of the structure originally established which seems therefore to have been 'dissolved' by progressive negations in a Hegelian sense.

Heinz-Kloll Metzge
DGG Record Sleeve
Prelude for String Quartet by Toshiro Mayuzumi

The Ravel *Rapsodie* made a supreme showpiece for the Chicago. Giulini milked it, with slow tempi squeezed to silken threads, and rhythms of narcissistic flexibility.

Gillian Widdicombe *Financial Times*

Pollini more than lived up to his reputation as a Chopin interpreter in the second set of Twelve Studies, op. 25: a feast of soft accents versus hard (No. 3), dramatic variations of tone-colour (No. 7), virtuosity suborbinated to musical ends

(Nos. 11 and 12): throughout a sense that the pianist's hands were no longer stupidly separate, their tune or accompaniment contributions being constantly blurred. After three encores, I fled. It was corrupting.

Meirion Bowen *Guardian*

At last a German composer has leapt the barrier that separates music lovers from the rest: Dr. Dieter Schneibe, a 38-year old Protestant pastor and musical theorist from the Black Forest, has written a work for conductor without orchestra which had its first performance recently in Germany. . . . .

One of his recent choral works is a "hymn of praise" consisting mainly of the tape-recorded cries of donkeys, apes, seagulls, dogs, cats, sheep, horses, cattle, parrots, bees, ducks, elephants, lions and turkeys.

Schnebel, who is a convinced Marxist and a strong supporter of West Germany's rebellious left-wing students, has also managed to introduce politics into his sacred music. At the climax of the "hymn", a voice emerges from the indescribable tumult of animal noises, shouting repeatedly "Ho, ho, ho". It is left to the singers to ad lib additional words – possibly Chi Minh.

The Diary *The Times*

HANS KELLER MEMORIAL PAGE

NONO. It is a sign of the times that *Il Canto Sospeso* (1956), though something of a contemporary classic, has never yet been performed in this country. What is elementally fruitful about Nono's talent is its lack of education. The absence of a secure background makes talented people either go wild (Cage), or tame, or a good deal of both: Nono. He tames his imagination vigorously, to the extent of employing a rhythmic series in this work which adds one consecutive integer after another to the successive values, the basic value being

2 + 0 = 2	5 + 3 = 8
2 + 1 = 3	8 + 4 = 12
3 + 2 = 5	12 + 5 = 17

Can you hear it? No. But it supports and relaxes him: now he can go wild without screaming.

Hans Keller *The Listener*

Invert all three axioms of conceptual reasoning and you have the axioms of musical thought – at any rate, inasmuch as it aims at communication. The Law of Identity says that A is A. When A remains A in a musical argument, nothing is said: the argument is circular, corresponding to a petitio principii *or* circulus in probando *in conceptual thought. It is a musical axiom that A must become more than A. The Law of Contradiction says that A is not both B and not B: in music it must, axiomatically, be both. The Law of Excluded Middle says that A either is or is not B, whereas in music it goes without saying that A must have it both ways if it is to be meaningful.*

Hans Keller *The Listener*

OBITUARY

British political life will be the poorer for the loss of Robert Arthur Gascoyne-Cecil, fifth Marquess of Salisbury, who has died aged 78.

Since the Cecils made such a tremendous intellectual come-back at the turn of the century, they have produced scions with minds like razors, with exquisitely sensitive souls, and with rugged opinions, the whole encased in curiously frail-looking corporeal tenements.

Colin R. Coote *Daily Telegraph*

It is fitting that the famous French writer, Henry de Montherlant, should have put an end to his life on Thursday by shooting himself through the head.

John Weightman *Observer*

Marc

PAINTING

Objects appear often in Vermeer's works. But they are generally containers - glasses or jugs. And the room in which Vermeer sets his figures are like containers too. The containers are hollow vessels from which vital essences (wine, water, milk) can be poured from one container to another. Human beings themselves are containers (in this sense, we are objects), into which things can be poured (wine, water, milk, sperm, words) and from which things may be poured (milk, sperm, blood, words). The objects in Vermeer's paintings are extensions of the people themselves.

Paul Overy (sic) *New Society*

Annigoni dipped a brush into water and damped the edge of the robes. Immediately the picture became alive and Annigoni promptly agreed to varnish it. "It was the most magical moment," says Dr (Roy) Strong, "it wasn't a portrait any more, it was a sensational experience."

Timothy Giles *Sunday Times*

My youngest animal image was painted as recently as two years ago – a large black tom-cat by the London painter Fred Aris. In art jargon, Aris, who is the proprietor of a small cafe in Dulwich, would be referred to as a Naive Painter, but there is nothing naive about his knowledge of that cat. It is a super-cat, almost more cat-like than a real cat. There it sits, waiting and watching for something exciting to happen. Well fed and well cared for, but with its biological urges strangely unsatisfied, it somehow symbolises in a completely non-anthropomorphic way the modern human dilemma of affluent urban man.

Desmond Morris *Observer Magazine*

Lord Beaumont agrees: "Any really good painting must say something to you immediately, and later you discover it has layers of meaning. This one has a tremendously powerful first impact. I'm not quite certain how much more it does say, what the other layers are. But I haven't got tired of the top layer yet."

Nigel Gosling *Observer Colour Mag*

The National Council for Civil Liberties has joined the fight to have eight American magazines returned to David Hockney, the painter. Mr. Hockney was deprived of the books by a customs official at London Airport on December 2, and although he has supplied a letter from Mr Norman Reid, the director of the Tate Gallery, explaining the connexion between the magazines and his work as an artist who is often concerned with the nude figure, he has since received neither an apology nor the magazines.

These were bought on general sale in New York and the titles, as Mr Hockney remembers them, included *Teenage Nudist*, *Male Nudist* and *Golden Boy*.

The Times Diary

Upstairs are two very large recent pictures which push the same idea further. Here he simply draws a line of black around the perimeter of the canvas, leaving the centre empty. Yet the space is so well judged that it feels oddly alive. It seems to give out something like the warmth of a chair which has been sat in: you feel a presence there, though only a formal one; we are near to that famous description of "drawing a line round a thought."

Nigel Gosling *The Observer*

Ever since Seurat, painters have known that certain angles – certain deviations from the horizontal – correspond to specific emotional states. There is an angle which recurs over and over in Caro. It measures about 105 degrees, and in all the books it is the standard way of keeping the lines open and saying "Yes" to life. It is by doing this, in the work, that Caro has found metaphors for just about everything from the pure festivity of "Month of May" (1963) to the suggestion, in "After Summer" (1968), that the whole earth is about to open up and a completely new universe come into being. It is something that belongs to the 1960's, and could not have been done earlier; the time and the man are one. John Russell *The Sunday Times*

In Tundra, *and in Newman's next two paintings, he seems to have been working towards the idea of presenting a square within a rectangle, but in such a way that the square would be invisible – a further variation and complication of his secret symmetry.*

Thomas B. Hess on Barnet Newman

POETRY

He (Christopher Logue. Ed). *has also just published his long poem* Girls *in a separate edition. Full of rhythms of water, of the sounds and light and heat of summer, it has an extraordinary brilliance of imagery. He originally wanted to bind it in "panties but couldn't find any made of strong enough material", but now it is bound in Liberty silk, and is available in a limited edition of 50 at £30 each from Bernard Stone, Kensington Church Walk, W.8.* Marina Warner *Vogue*

Belli's poems communicate to us not only much more of his own satirical bitterness, but also of the whole flavour and mood of living in nineteenth-century Rome rather than elsewhere and in another age, whereas a similar Haiku remains almost rootless both in time and space and tells us much less about the poet himself:

A horse farts:
Four or five suffer
On the ferry-boat.

Has any New York poet, riding the subway during the rush hour, ever been inspired to as pungent an epigram on the inconveniences of living in the lonely crowd?

Edouard Roditi *London Magazine*

LOVE SONG

Mabel was a
Table

Lovely table

On the table
(Mabel)

Lay a flower
Named Cyril.

Barry Daniels *Encounter*

Ninhursag seated Enki by her pudendum,
"My brother, what hurts you?"
"My . . . hurts me."

(Translated by S. N. Kramer from the Sumerian poem "Enki and Ninhursag.")

To the enthusiastic but non-specialised student of the Sumerians, these lines – and in particular, the three dots which are such a significant part of them – epitomise the enigma of that remote and fascinating people. What, we ask, is going on here? Who are this couple? What is the missing word? Is it unfit to print? Or has the translator met with a genuine difficulty in deciphering the original? Indeed, the impression made on the reader is an ambivalent one, recalling the effect of the nursery rhyme, Jack and Jill, when punctuated in a similar fashion:

Jack and Jill went up the hill
To . . .
Jack fell down and . . .
And Jill . . . James Wellard *Encounter*

A gigantic Danish whore once told me in Paris that she had just passed the night with a man who was so small that she simply couldn't find him in the bed in the morning – she looked everywhere. And it occurs to me now that he must have been Baudelaire because of those lines in 'La Geante'. Dormir nonchalamment a l'ombre de ses seins comme un hameau paisible au pied d'une montaigne.

Richard Buckle *Sunday Times*

Robert Harris blows up balloons in Rochdale Art Gallery on Saturday mornings. It's part of a series of events organised by the Axis group of poets. The balloons have words on them. Like "Blow-up". "I'm interested in words", Mr Harris says, "and making people aware how the meaning of words depends on the words on either side. So one balloon begins: 'Hello, I'm crazy' and expands to say 'about you'."

Mr Harris, who studied architecture, and used to be assistant stage manager to Northern Dance Theatre, got into balloons because he found ordinary poetry readings so boring. *Guardian*

POP

The experience of listening to rock music is the experience of putting one's sensibility in flux.

Geoffrey Cannon *The Guardian*

One of the most disconcerting moments in Pink Floyd's *Ummagumma* (double album, Harvest, 59s 11d) occurs when someone crosses the room to swat a buzzing fly. Since the action is isolated, it is easily placed in space. His footsteps are gradually phased from one speaker to the other and simultaneously brought closer to the microphone (i.e. you). The effect is to trace a diagonal line of approach towards the listener who is then swatted. (On second thoughts, like Pozzo's St Ignazio ceiling, perhaps it only works if you are in the correct position.) *Spectator*

Pink Floyd are the ultimate statement about why I believe in pop music. Last night they played for an hour a new piece The Dark Side of the Moon *that brought tears to the eyes. It was so completely understanding and musically questioning.*

Michael Wale *Times*

Jagger is rather like Dostoevsky's Brother Karamazov who, when told by his venerable brother that pain must exist so that we might learn of goodness, replied that if it was necessary that one small child should suffer in order that he should be made more aware, he did not deny the existence of God, but merely respectfully returned his ticket of admission to Heaven.

That is Mick Jagger's kind of rebellion.

Keith Altham *Melody Maker*

As musical sage and mentor John Peel has said, it is not easy to write objectively about Bridget St John. Hearing or speaking with her, however, is "as good as renting a cottage by the sea."

Yes indeed. Her voice is a feminine synthesis of the four elements, a natural, unpretentious voice, autumnal, husky but smooth, with the plaintiveness of a forest waterfall, the purity of the wind in the hedgerows, the earthiness of the vapours that rise from peat in the early morning.

G.F. *South Westerner*

A competitor in what he calls "the great beard race," he stands on stage arms flailing, head shaking, hair whipping his sweating face, his gusty, dirty voice like a bull-dozer crashing through a brick wall at 90 miles an hour. Cocker looks like a creature demented, ploughing through Dylan's "Dear Landlord," and Ray Charles' invitation to "Let's Go Get Stoned." He announces "This is one of George Harrison's hits" and sings a song he recorded ages ago, a song from his next album, a song called "Something." He's too bloody much. That's all.

B P Fallon *Melody Maker*

And the characteristic mode of determinism is not investigation by criticism, but justification by description: an intellectual mode which might just as well be called anti-intellectual, since no matter how much information it aspires to deal with it can never arrive at a judgement. The rock culture grew up in a mental vacuum; and the fact that it grew at all - and grew so fast - was in itself sufficient proof of the aesthetic truism that creativity is a primal urge, antecedent to rational mentality.

Clive James *Cream*

As she sang, her nose looked very like that of Bob Dylan.

Geoffrey Cannon *Grauniad*

Just after midnight, a piece of masonry fell off the top of the Cafe Tingis onto the head of one of the waiters, who crashed to the ground, his metal tray and glasses of milk and hot coffee miraculously going down with him and not spilling. He was taken inside and a week later he was still going round with a bandage on his head, looking nervous and shaken. "I love to see things falling apart," said Seymour. "It's the decay which keeps me coming back here." It was probably the huge lumps of majoung we had eaten earlier in the evening but the incident suddenly seemed symbolic of the decline and fall of all western civilisation. Jim Anderson *Oz*

POLITICS

People like Geoffrey Crowther come rarely to lift men's eyes towards new goals. *Economist*

Sir Alec is a modest man—speaking of himself as "one" rather than "I"—with the unpretentious good manners of the old nobility.

Kenneth Young *Here Come the Tories*

Shaw admits to some incongruity in a Socialist enjoying the comforts of the Savoy and talking about his wealth. He says that it is a dilemma that has confronted him for some time, but he has reconciled himself to it in the knowledge that he is an autocrat and does not know a talented person who is not. "Here I am living like a capitalist and yet I believe that if there were a real chance of equality of opportunity, of real socialism, then I would give up all the money. It would all go. Definitely, definitely, definitely. That I really feel."

Robert Shaw talking to Terry Philpott
Grauniad

The need for cannabis and the need for other forms of artificial stimulation of that kind is essentially the product of authoritarianism and in this case a capitalist society.

Peter Hain *Daily Telegraph*

RELIGION

By this time Jesus has come to dread the Messianic fate he has courted, but his power grows with his vulnerability. "Don't worry about it, Judas," he says later, after the kiss in the garden; and to Pilate in the examination – the finest scene of all – "Don't be afraid". (This really frightens Pilate, who has already been startled by the scourged prophet's first words on having his blindfold removed: "Good afternoon." It was such an extraordinary remark in the circumstances that the tears leapt from my eyes.)

John Holmstrom *New Statesman*

Rev. Dick York, Berkely Free Church, is due here this month and wants to meet English radical Christians. He will break bread and speak with us at a special liberation eucharist. Sounds, songs, percussion, ritual, OM, liberation chants. Union Church, Ponds Sq., Highgate.

Advertisement *The Catonsville Roadrunner*

The infant daughter of Mr and Mrs Robin Thistlethwayte was christened Sophia Mary Clare by the Rev. T. A. Wharton at St. Mary's church, Chipping Norton, on Sunday, July 2. The godparents are Lieutenant-Colonel Noel Thistlethwayte, Captain Jonathan Hok, the Hon. Mrs Peter Trustram Eve and Miss Madeleine Drage.

The Times

. . . there is the danger for the Festival of Light that, in the process of institutionalisation, it will alienate the charismatically-motivated youthful wing, who have so far provided its dynamic quality. As they turn to more immediately experiential modes of witness, they may take with them any current emphasis on humanitarian

and democratic pluralism, and leave behind the coercive reformism and unalleviated moral indignation of a status-declining middle class.

Roy Wallis *New Society*

This obsession with religiosity is also a recurring theme in the first Monty Python film, *And Now For Something Completely Different*, now showing in London. Nowhere is it more explicit than in the story of the man who returns to a pet shop with a deceased parrot. He claims the shopkeeper has sold him "a pup." In fact, it's neither a bird nor a dog. It is, of course, a symbol, a cinematic metaphor for God. It's a parable on contemporary society in which God, Christianity and Jesus Christ have all disappeared from mass consciousness. God is dead, the Monty Python team is saying. Man must strive to regain the animal instinctiveness that is buried beneath the weight of cultural sophistication.

Michael Watts *Melody Maker*

A nude girl is hung upside down being threatened with a razor. Author Dr. Francis Williams explains: "The scene is an attempt to convey the immediacy of a religious experience in the most basic terms."

Scottish Daily Express on 'Lying Figures' at the Edinburgh Festival Fringe

---

SEX

The erection of a penis is in itself a piece of natural mechanism of great interest and of human significance.

George Melly *The Observer*

He (Alan Sekers) is not a man who finds it easy to do nothing. His conversation crackles with energy, lavishly spiced with explicit sexual imagery. He has, nevertheless, the curiously aseptic sexuality of so many of today's swinging young Londoners. He is indifferent to the taboos of middle-aged society, finding in sex a purity and beauty that they miss.

Recently he worked on a project at the Round House in which the patterns of electrical brain activity from a man and a girl (hitherto total strangers) making love were projected onto a vast 180° screen. "It was beautiful" he recalls. "We had abstracted just this one precise part of the act of love and shown it absolutely straight and unadorned. It was so pure it was marvellous." It wasn't phoney or daring or trendy when be described it. He meant it.

Fashion

The author of this unusual study of "homosexual encounters in public places" is a minister of religion turned sociologist currently Assistant Professor at the University of Southern Illinois. He does not attempt to test any hypothesis but is clearly influenced by Goffman. After a preliminary year of intensive observation, he witnessed some 120 sexual acts in 19 different lavatories in five parks of one city. He then concentrated on one particular park lavatory and by passing himself off as a deviant and acting as look-out man, made systematic observations on homosexual encounters there.

He was able to integrate his research sample into a much wider social health survey after identifying the subjects by tracing their car licence numbers. This enabled him to interview them personally and complete a questionnaire. The bulk of the book consists of a detailed analysis of 50 deviants (from an original sample of 134) and a matched control group obtained from the same health survey. F E Kenyon

British Journal of Psychiatry, No. 552

The engraving on glass of the Somerset church of St. Julian, Wellow, depicted in The Times *yesterday, was the work of Mr David H Maude-Roxby-Montalto di Fragnito.*

The Times

Later, in the restaurant, he leaned over to a lady, and said, "Do you know the most erotic part of your body?" Longish pause. He drew a little circle in his palm. "There." He took her hand, enclosing it, and drew a little circle in her palm. Later, after we parted from Lomax, she said, "I'm afraid he's quite right. I never knew." Geoffrey Cannon

(on Alan Lomax) *Grauniad*

It has been asserted that by cutting down the bean-stalk Jack castrates either his father or else himself in order to escape the pursuing Oedipal hostility of the giant. To quote Richard Forson, surely the best writer on international folklore today, "the analysts do agree that the beanstalk is a penis: the question is, whose?"

Nicholas Tucker *New Society*

Nicholas, the charming bisexual failure, in love with youth wherever it can be persuaded to raise its ugly head in order to admire him, observes his brother's spiral towards suicide with a kind of unembittered irony that remains attractive even when it gets a bit facile round the edges. Caroline, married to a psychiatrist, worries mostly about her daughter Anne, a would-be Lady Macbeth, stern and intense, given to erotic fantasies in which she poisons chaps with ice-cream.

All three principal characters are much concerned with their relationship to the now-dead father. When Nicholas – in a very strong scene – discovers from an aunt that the father was impotent, and they are someone else's children, the spell is too strict to be broken. Isn't the aunt lesbian, and doesn't her story of having maimed her brother on a breakwater sound like a classic case of penis envy?

Mr Ramsbotham's theme, it will be apparent, is sex as a source of confusion. He treats it with a wit which is lucid and ambiguous at one and the same time, so that one recalls Charles Lamb's interesting remark about the possibility of obscurity through too much meaning.

Robert Nye *Guardian*

---

*When a television programme (*Horizon, *BBC2) can say that a male has an 'erection usually a little faster than the female lubricates,' something important has happened.*

Christopher Ricks *The Listener*

It is of great significance that at last a British geriatrician has written a book on sex in old age.

World Medicine

Once all the ambiguities have been severely scrutinized and discarded, once this notion of structure has been purified of all the metaphysical and substantialist contents that it was at risk of keeping hidden within itself, it is not utopian to speak of the proximity of a specific structural epistemology; the very possibility of building a system of all the possible variations of this concept "structure" is now at hand, and one would undertake the construction of a formal network, a sort of neo-Leibnitzian organon which would comprehend the structural genesis of every possible operation related to the use of systems or models, not only in the two major fields of mathematics and linguistics whence structural methods were first originated, but covering also all the so-called "empirical" fields of culture with formalized "local" networks, the specificity of which would have not only to be formally active at the first degree, but also capable of speaking critically of themselves in a formalized structural language: structuralist as well as metastructuralist activities would be able to find a genuine and formal location on this general network of relationships, on this displayed formal mobile set of exchange and communication which would characterize epistemology and science nowadays, following the example of mathematics since Bourbaki.

Jean-Marie Benoist *Cambridge Review*

TV AND RADIO

Let's come to the next flashpoint. Sex. I'd like to put the proposition to you that being a single person in a room with a radio set is like being in bed with someone. It's essentially an erotic situation.

Michael Kustow *Radio Times*

The producer (of the *Black and White Minstrel Show*), Ernest Maxin, confesses an emotional involvement that's unusual among professionals. "When I watch the finished show in the control box I'm tremendously moved by it," he says. "Even to tears."

Jenny Campbell *Radio Times*

So once again the dear, maligned, unpredictable BBC gave us a play that made one proud to have a television set. I confess that I wept for the tender beauty, the humour and the sadness of this one. And I do not care who knows.*

Leonard Buckley *The Times*

Decisions, decisions. There have been a few painful ones this week. How to choose on Monday night, for instance, between Malraux's *La Condition Humaine* dramatised on Radio 4, the Bach *B minor Mass* relay from St Paul's cathedral on Radio 3, and *Doddy's Half-hour* on Radio 2.

Gillian Reynolds *The Guardian*

THEATRE

When Bury and Hall worked together on The Homecoming, *they realised that the apples in a bowl that constituted part of the set had to be green. Red ones would not do, and even the green ones they had for the New York production weren't quite right; too big, practically the size of grapefruit.* Michael McNay *Guardian*

---

* *Lady Windermere's Fan*

***The Boyfriend* is a disease, a putrescent effluence of garbage encouraging and reinforcing all the most negative modes of existence.**

Time Out

Except for one sudden flurry of excited question-marks (and one question-mark elsewhere which wasn't part of the punctuation of Beckett's French text, *Le Depeupleur*, and which ought surely to be reconsidered), the only punctuation is the full-stop. What a haggard stoical gait that gives to Beckett's prose, never to indulge in a comma or dash or semi-colon or colon. His style stiffens towards death; his full-stops, daunting but undaunted, take up all his time and space. His, and ours. Time must have a stop.

Christopher Ricks *The Sunday Times*

The inter-relation existing between the convention of language and the rule of morality is a field in which ambiguity can be used to advantage by anybody concerned with the arts. Thus, a writer who wants to alter the structure of morality can do so by containing his polemic in a syntax which is, in itself, an alteration, an alteration to the structure of language that runs parallel to moral structure. His obscenities will surmount morality that much more effectively if they take place without sentence, plot or any other normal linguistic setting.

Jeff Nuttall

Traverse Theatre Club Programme

"The 'Ugly Duckling' is very loaded towards a hierarchical Fascist kind of society: the duckling doesn't just become a duck, it becomes a swan."

Anthony Storey *Grauniad*

Three Reviews by Harold Hobson

(Sunday Times)

This central theme is embroidered with all kinds of baroque decorations. Why does Alice scream after cunnilingus? Why in the libation scene does the lawyer not touch his champagne? What is the meaning of the endearments between the lawyer and the butler? Why is Alice not merely outrageously wealthy, but wealthy beyond all human possibility? What really happened during Julian's six years in the asylum to which he fled when he lost his faith? Did anything happen at all? What is the meaning of the fading of the lights in the model chapel? Is it damnation? Or, since the chapel is an evil place, is it the contrary of damnation? These questions constantly stimulate the dramatic interest, and it is altogether in line with contemporary man's recognition.

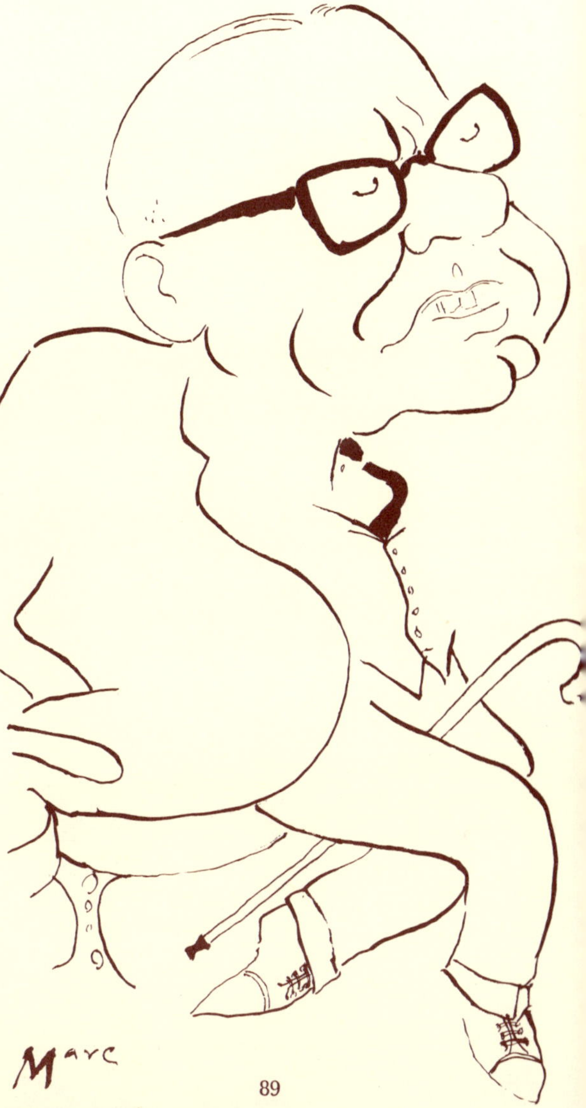

In the celebrated scene with Barnadine, the drunken prisoner who refuses to be executed on the grounds that he is not in a fit state to enter the next world, Mr Barton carries this attack to its penultimate stage. He causes Barnadine to urinate into a pot, into which a crucifix is then thrown. This desecration is followed by the crucifix and the urine, a thick, yellow stream, being poured over Barnadine's head as he disappears. I suggest that the point of this scene would be greatly strengthened if the urine were not Barnadine's, but Isabella's.

The Mousetrap, for example, is no ordinary thriller, to be dismissed as an entertainment for thickheads. From the critical point of view its whole significance lies in its symbolism. It embodies, in an exciting story, more vividly than scores of intellectually pretentious plays, the central tragedy of our time, which is the almost complete collapse of all our certainties, political, social, economic, and religious. The climax of the play comes, in a pin-point of really remarkable intensity, with the instant destruction of the most solid of our convictions. Dramatists, when truly inspired, often write beyond the limit of their conscious intention. *The Mousetrap* is as much a parable of our times as *The Pilgrim's Progress* was of the seventeenth century.

ENCOUNTERS

The first thing you notice about Anna Calder Marshall is the way she speaks. Words come in slow drawn out, clearly consonated, deep breaths, tied into lugubrious gurgled sentences by chains of pauses, while she stares you straight in the eyes, unblinking, and I suspect, unseeing.

Ask her a question, any old ordinary question, such as "When did you last sleep nude?", and she practically goes into deep meditation in her effort to think out, and give you the most accurate possible answer.

"Whenever it was last hot enough," she finally comes up with, and the agony of intensity arrests her eyes and my eyes, and then we both breathe again in mutual relief.

Ray Connolly *Evening Standard*

Noel Coward did not say 'I wrote *Private Lives* in Shanghai very quickly,' but 'I wrote *Private Lives* in Shanghai' - fractional pause - 'very' - even more fractional pause - 'quickly.' It was the perfectly judged caesura which lightly flicked my funnybone . . .

Patrick Garland *The Observer*

I was aware of a slight trembling of his head and hands as he bit into a Cox's Orange Pippin. This trembling gave the impression not of infirmity, but of the vibration of a powerful intellectual machine.

Richard Kennedy on Leonard Woolf
Sunday Times Magazine

It was my privilege to sit next to M. (Andre) Simon. I had been looking forward to talking to him and it was, therefore, to say the least, disconcerting, to find that almost in mid-sentence he had gone to sleep.

Was it because the circadian rhythm of a nonagenarian had been disturbed by a plethora of air travel? Was it fatigue or was I being a bore? Eventually he opened his eyes, took a sip of wine and said quite simply, "There is so much". I have never been quite sure what he meant by this, but I rather think that he was telling me in quite a Gallic way that moderation and quality was, from an eubiotic point of view, preferable to an over-abundant superfluity.

G. R. Davidson *Guardian*

In the kitchen Joan (Bakewell) picks up a tray on which there are two cups and saucers, with coffee dripping through those little tin hats the French use and which, somehow, tell you a lot about a person – and sometimes are meant to. As we move out of the kitchen the housekeeper very sensibly asks: 'Do you want some milk?' and Joan replies – as if there was never any question – 'No'. Then a second later, 'Do you take milk?' and I say, heaven knows why, 'No', even though I do, I *do*. It's that kind of effect that Joan Bakewell has on many men.

Douglas Keay *Cosmopolitan*

The bullet holes make a disagreeable pattern across a wall of the flat Nicol Williamson rents from a sheikh in the Via Dolorosa within the walls of the Old City. The prophet Isaiah once lived down the road. Directly across from the flat is Pontius Pilate's courtyard where Jesus was sentenced.

Williamson, shoulders hunched in the characteristic way, stands on the roof in the darkness under a star-crossed Heaven. He looks around at the skyline of the Holy City, the Dome of the Rock (where Solomon built his Temple) dominating the mosques, churches, cypresses and the rows of TV aerials, and he mutters, "Extraordinary. It shifts your guts."

Sydney Edwards *Evening Standard*

LORD GOODMAN

I don't know much about cars but I have no difficulty in recognising the quality of a Rolls-Royce. Similarly I recognise the beauty of Lord Goodman's mind. It is a pleasure to watch him think.

Jennie Lee *Daily Telegraph Magazine*

It is the superlative ease, the unruffled assurance with which that mind works which first impresses those who meet him. One can hardly hear the mechanism working at all and yet the results have a perfect precision. Without any sense of strain or pretension that marvellous instrument absorbs all the arguments presented to it and sifts from them an endless flow of conclusions framed in smooth, yet vibrant English.

Michael Foot *Evening Standard*

There are people who are chosen to fill an historic need. Winston Churchill was such a one. Perhaps Lord Goodman is another.

Harold Rubinstein
Daily Telegraph Magazine

As he enters the party, like a tanker edging towards her moorings, bonhomie, goodwill, warmth, friendliness, even a touch of fantasy radiate through the room. People perk up and look happier. He menaces no-one: that is why politicians like him.

Lord Annan *The Times*

All myths explore the richness of systematic ambiguity.

Geoffrey Cannon
The Guardian

THE END

Selected and introduced by Richard Ingrams.
Re-shaped by Andrew Osmond.